Rea McDonnell, S.S.N.D.
and
Rachel Callahan, C.S.C.

W9-CAA-174

Hope for Healing

Good News for
Adult Children of Alcoholics

Paulist Press
New York • Mahwah

also by Rea McDonnell, S.S.N.D.
published by Paulist Press
PRAYER PILGRIMAGE THROUGH SCRIPTURE
PRAYER PILGRIMAGE WITH PAUL

Photo Credits

Step One: Awareness
Jagdish Agarwal
Step Two: Discipleship
Bob & Miriam Francis
Step Three: Conversion
Gene Plaisted

Step Four: Community
Cleo Freelance Photo
Step Five: Union
Dale G. Folstad
Step Six: Forgiveness
Christian Rohlfs, Collection
The Museum of Modern Art, New York

Library of Congress Cataloging-in-Publication Data

McDonnell, Rea.
    Hope for healing : good news for adult children of alcoholics /
Rea McDonnell and Rachel Callahan.
    p.   cm.
    Bibliography: p.
    ISBN 0-8091-2929-9 (pbk.) : $4.95
    1. Adult children of alcoholics—Religious life.   I. Callahan,
Rachel.   II. Title.
BV4596.A27M37 1987
248.8'6—dc19

Published by Paulist Press
997 Macarthur Blvd.
Mahwah, N.J. 07430

Printed and bound in the United States of America

Contents

*Dedicated
to our fathers,
John and Ed*

Prologue

Our book, offering six steps in and toward the grace of healing for adult children of alcoholics, is based on an image from Ireland.

Several years ago, I visited Killarney. My companions and I came upon an ancient, walled-in cemetery at the top of the hill at Agadhoe. There seemed no way into this enclosure of old ruins until one of my friends, a native Irish woman, spotted a stile. "A stile?" I puzzled. As she clambered over the set of steps, leading the way, she pointed out footholds in the wall. We climbed over, expecting to see some interesting tombstones. I was surprised, overcome by a vista of the lakes of Killarney.

On this bright, sunny day it was heart-scaldingly beautiful. Looking out at the scene—glistening lakes, rain-nourished greens, even barren stones, I cried, thinking of the beauty my ancestors left (but as my Irish friend commented, "You can't eat beauty"). The stile had brought us to the place of death *and* beauty, of light and roots. We needed the footholds it provided to enter this place.

Hopefully this book will provide some footholds for the adult child(ren) of alcoholics (ACOA) which will help you scale some walls, fears, defenses, hostilities. You may think you are climbing a fence around death and its remains, but hopefully you will discover the "terrible beauty" of your own self and your roots and the God who is named (among many other names) Rock and Strong-hold.

May God grasp you with a "strong hold" as you climb over this wall.

Introduction

We offer not handholding but footholds, steps in and toward grace, for adult children of alcoholics, for anyone whom the disease of alcoholism has damaged and who now wants God's healing. Within that sentence are embedded three hurdles for many of us who have grown up within a Christian tradition. Let us try to transform hurdles to stiles.

The first hurdle is the nature of alcoholism itself. Alcoholism is a disease. It is not sin, nor a failure of will power. The second hurdle is denial. We may have lived a lifetime of pain and denial of our wounds, sometimes not even knowing whether our parent(s) truly might be alcoholic. The third hurdle is our perception of God. So many of us desperately prayed that our parent(s) would stop drinking. No matter how hard we worked to please God, the God we addressed abandoned us. We could not trust our parents, nor ourselves, nor, many of us, even God.

Alcoholism Is a Disease

Alcoholism is not a sin. Most adult children of alcoholics in their forties, fifties or sixties were taught just that, however, at least by osmosis at parish missions or revivals. Not long ago, a sixty year old man, noted for his piety, asked, "Won't my

3

wife be damned to hell and won't I be held responsible for her damnation?'' In this book we will work with images of sin and grace, images of God and salvation which, scripturally based as they are, should correct such misconceptions and help heal such spiritual terror.

Alcoholism is not a failure of will power. Alcoholics themselves most often have an alcoholic parent, come from what we would call an alcoholic home. Their own parents or grandparents may have modeled escaping from pain, or abusing spouse or children. Will power, however, can no more heal the alcoholic than it can heal cancer or pneumonia or diabetes. As it was taught in the past, spirituality often meant will power for holiness, a practice of virtue. Emotions were suspect. We, however, will use scripture to understand spirituality as a robust, emotional attachment to God.

Alcoholism is a disease. Diabetes may offer a good comparison. It runs in families. It can be controlled but never conquered. Until it is faced and dealt with, diabetes can cause havoc within the person and within the person's network of relationships. Hiding out from diabetes can cause death. Denying alcoholism can lead to physical death and has probably led to all manner of psychospiritual death among the family members. Just as once we didn't want to hear about cancer, avoided visiting cancer patients, etc. (and now it is AIDS), it is not easy, even now, to hear about alcoholism. We are not alone. If you have read this far, God is blessing your desire for healing and giving you the Spirit of truth.

Truth after a Lifetime of Denial

The Holy Spirit of truth has guided and will guide us ever deeper into truth. We are not alone in our long-term denial, blocking memories, blotting out pain. There are some constants about alcoholic families, and denial of painful realities is probably chief. Even as you read this book, we ask you to beg the Spirit of truth to help you not deny reality, neither the past nor the present. Pray as simply as this, each time you turn a page, before each exercise:

Holy Spirit of truth, set me free!

This Holy Spirit will not destroy you nor lead you into too much truth too fast. Like a gentle breeze, the Spirit will gradually open up for you that truth, that memory, that reality which will gradually transform death into new life, pain into new power.

Besides this Holy Spirit, you may need a very human support person during this time of discovery. Ideally a spouse (who is not presently chemically addicted) or a friend or a sibling can listen to you, pray with you. ACOA groups modeled on Alcoholics Anonymous, Al Anon and Ala-teen are available almost everywhere and are a structure of grace, for grace in our society. Group counseling or personal therapy may help. One woman religious, after two years of daily praying to the Spirit of truth, "Don't let me deny," was ready for therapy. "I have years of tears," she explained to her spiritual director, "and I don't want to drown my community in them. At least a therapist will know how to swim." This woman had denied pain most of her life. A priest friend had alerted her: "If you don't let yourself feel, really feel the dying, you'll miss so much of the joy of resurrection."

Two particular denials plague the ACOA. First, we may not yet admit even to ourselves that there was abuse of alcohol in our home. Perhaps we thought our home was normal, yet guarding the family secret made us question what "normal" really meant. Sometimes, many times, only when we ask clients or directees directly will they admit to the secret they have kept for twenty or forty or sixty years. The second common denial is that the non-drinking parent could have any flaw at all. We will pay attention to the ACOA tendency to all or nothing thinking and to the idol-making in which we all engage.

If you are still reading, thank the Spirit for guiding you to truth about yourself and your parent.

> Thank you, Holy Spirit, gentle counselor,
>   for opening up deeper truth within me.
> Melt the frozen; warm the chill;
>   light the darkness; what's empty, fill.

Finally, in begging the Spirit to melt and warm, we will discover how frozen, buried, many of our emotions are. Emotions are God's creation and thus they are good. Yet we have been taught to deny at least certain feelings, either because strong emotions would upset the tenuous peace in the house or because emotions such as anger, hatred, revenge, and fear were taught to us at home, school and church as sinful. When we are consoled, reading about God in the gentle breeze:

> The Lord was not in the wind . . .
> The Lord was not in the earthquake . . .
> The Lord was not in the fire . . . (1 Kgs 19:10–18)

we continue to read that God's voice in the gentle breeze instructed Elijah to anoint revengers so that everyone who had worshiped idols would be slain! We will look at *every* emotion as God's gift to us and we will especially treat of "tough love."

We Want God's Healing

We have always wanted healing—healing for the alcoholic. Most of us were not "answered" by God but (1) even if our parent(s) stopped drinking, alcoholic behavior may have continued; (2) even if they turned their lives over to God through the AA community and program, some damage has been done.

Now that we are adults, perhaps grasping more fully the nature of the disease, we want healing for ourselves. Yet it is a risk to want, to want anything from anybody, even from God. We cushion our prayers with "not my will but your will be done, God." Most often we can't let even God know how hungry we are, how deep our desires, how desperate our longing for belonging, approval, control, affection. Sometimes work or chocolate or computers or sleep or sex or even the hated alcohol itself substitutes for the deeper hungers of our hearts.

Once there was a woman in Samaria who hungered for husbands. She took what she wanted and was still unsatisfied. Then Jesus asked her, "Give me a drink." In that scene, Jesus cut through her denial of pain and her diversion of desire. "I would give you enough life deep within your very self," he promised, "that you would never be thirsty again" (Jn 4:4–34).

> Holy Spirit, welling up from deep within us, we trust your presence and your power. We are hungry and thirsty for your healing. Be our fountain of never failing water, be our life in abundance (Jn 7:37–39; 10:10).

Remember, if it is difficult to pray that prayer of trust, that thousands of ACOA are finding the same difficulty, but are praying with you. Moreover, Jesus himself stands before the face of God making intercession for us (Heb 7:20). As he proclaimed at the end of the account of the Samaritan woman, Jesus' food and his drink, his most passionate desire, is to do what God wants. God wants our healing. And nothing is impossible to God.

Using This Book

Some practical suggestions for using this book: Go slowly. ACOA are often addicted to excitement, new ideas, adventure, working hard to achieve goals. Remember that God wants your healing so much more than you do, and God will not be controlled by your timetable. Pause often as you read to feel a feeling, relive a memory, breathe in the Spirit, breathe out some hostility. After feeling, reliving, breathing in or out, you might want to jot the feeling or memory in a journal kept right at hand with this book.

There are a number of workbooks for ACOA providing exercises for self-understanding. We, on the other hand, will offer both scripture-based exercises and prayers. Ours is a footbook, proposing six steps in and toward the grace, the healing, the wholeness that is God's *shalom,* God's passionate desire for us.

Our format was devised as we reflected on how a running sore or a wound might be healed. To know we are in pain is the first step toward healing. That *awareness* is a first step in and toward grace. Then we must be willing to discard the old remedies and dirty bandages that covered our wound. We will relearn some of the ways we related to our family, to God and to ourselves. To be a learner in Latin is to be a *discipulus/a,* the root of *discipleship,* our second step.

Central to healing is our change of mind and heart, our *conversion,* not our parent's. As a third step, we must be willing to go into the wound, the pain, to feel the astringent cleansing, seeping into most hidden parts. The agent of this healing, this conversion is the Spirit, the most gentle of healers. Exposing the wound to the light of Jesus and the fresh air of the

Spirit leads us to *community*, the fourth step, our need to share our woundedness with another or with a welcoming group. After so much probing, it is important to let the wound rest, letting re-creation happen from within; this step in and toward grace we call *union*. Finally, beginning and/or continuing our lifelong process of healing, we step in and toward grace, then out in *service*, letting the Spirit use us as instruments of healing for others.

Our prayer is that you may make the word of God your home; then you will know the truth and the truth will set you free (Jn 8:32).

Step One: Awareness

1. Step One: Awareness

Step one, in and toward grace: **Recognizing our wound and God's desire to heal.**

Rather than trying to describe awareness, we ask you to begin with an exercise to experience it. While not a verbal prayer, this is a first step in grace, toward grace, a way to let God's love wash over you, the Spirit to well up within every bone and muscle.

Sit in a comfortable chair, feet flat on the floor, back against the back of your chair. Close your eyes and breathe, deeply, slowly . . . inhale, exhale. Notice what you are feeling. As you focus your attention on the different parts of your body, be aware of the feelings, sensations: softness, hardness, tension, tiredness. Now, let's go a step further and imagine an interior space of relaxation, a space that is safe and as free from tension and anxiety as you have ever known. You can create this space any time you wish, and return to its safety at different times as you move through these steps.

First of all, as you are sitting (or lying) in a comfortable position systematically relax the different mus-

cles of your body. Start at your toes and work your
way up, tensing and relaxing each of the muscle
groups: toes, feet, calves, thighs, buttocks, back,
shoulder, neck, arms, hands, face, head. After you
gently tense and relax your whole body, create a fantasy for yourself of a place that is safe, relaxing,
soothing. It might be the beach, for example. Let
yourself feel the warmth of the sun, the gentle breeze
caressing every part of your body. Hear the
rhythmic, lapping, "shush-ing" sound of the waves.
And just relax, relax.

You have created your own "safe place." This relaxation
exercise is a technique available to you if painful feelings produce too much anxiety. Don't worry if you haven't been able
to "get into" this exercise. ACOA have invested much energy
in not feeling and in trying to contain some painful awareness.
Necessary for our survival as children, denying painful feelings has worked for us in the past and is not easily given up.

As part of our first step toward healing, awareness, we invite the Spirit to let us recognize some old wounds. Some
might have been inflicted so early in our lives that it's hard to
name them except by their pain. "I can't trust people." "I feel
that if I get close to someone, I will end up abandoned." We
will need the Spirit of truth to teach us, to open our memories—gently, over time.

We know from careful observational studies that the early
years of a child's mothering need to be, in David Winnicott's
expression, "good enough." Our infant needs for food and
soothing and maternal attention must be met with enough
consistency so that we start to experience people and the
world as trustworthy. If mother, however, is alcoholic herself,
she cannot meet these needs. If she is not herself alcoholic,
she is a co-dependent. Her focus on her spouse and her sub-

sequent worry and depression make her less emotionally available to the child. Co-dependent parents are just that, dependent on alcohol for their feelings, self-esteem; in other words, the life of the family is centered on the alcohol even if one parent is not alcoholic.

This early experience of deprivation leaves a child feeling abandoned and finally forces a child to deny his/her own need because the pain of abandonment is simply too great to bear. Like shrapnel, this pain opens many wounds: difficulties in trusting; difficulties maintaining realistic expectations of self and others; vulnerability to perceived threats of abandonment; an unsure sense of a real self. Unsure of the "real me," the child may grow too suggestible—continually trying to mold the clay of a public self to fit the needs and desires of the persons from whom the child wants love and approval. ACOA are very hungry for love and approval and care, although we may camouflage this well by becoming a super-nurturer ourselves, taking care of everyone else.

Super-nurturers look special: blessed with talents, responsible, serious. We make wonderful missionaries and ministers, parishioners generous with time and quick to take responsibility. We feel special to God too. What would God do without us? We are kingdom builders, although just whose kingdom we are creating blurs. We are earning God's love and approval, practicing virtue, winning merit. We have a right to God's blessing. In some churches, even recently, these feelings and behaviors were rewarded.

As that reward system begins to crumble, other difficulties in our spiritual life emerge. Starving for love, ACOA may find intimacy terrifying. Our difficulties with intimacy can be masked as detachment so that we may love God above all others. Difficulties with unrealistic expectations of self are camouflaged as "striving for perfection." Difficulties in trusting that God and the world are good simply encourage our pseudo-control of God and our attempt to manage our world. Self-awareness, however, alerts us to the underlying motivations of so many saintly looking behaviors. The Spirit begins to teach us truth that will allow us to be who we really are: frightened, angry, lonely creatures so incredibly loved by God.

Awareness That All Is Grace

Grace is translated in various ways. In the Jewish scriptures it is described as the *hesed* and *'emet* of God. Both are names for God's own self. *Hesed* means God's unconditional, abundant, extravagant love, tenderness, kindness, mercy. *'Emet* means God's unswerving, faithful, true, consistent and everlasting devotion to us. *Hesed* in Greek is *charis,* a free gift of God's unconditional love, a love faithful no matter how unfaithful we may be. No need to measure up, to win approval, to seek God's favor. The good news is that we are loved, right now, today, just as we are: faithfully and consistently loved, never to be abandoned—really—although sometimes feeling at a distance from such goodness.

To acknowledge that God wants to heal us may be so difficult if we think that God's will is for pain, suffering, even for the innocent Jesus in his tortured death. In chapter three we will look at Jesus' prayer for God's will to be done during/after his agony in the garden. In the next chapter, however, we will look at God's will for our healing and wholeness by re-examining some images of God. We will also reassess what it means to be human and what it means to be spiritual. Now, perhaps just by gritting our teeth and willing it, let us *try,* through this exercise, to acknowledge our pain and God's desire to heal us.

Because much of our woundedness stems from early childhood, perhaps even earlier than we can remember, let's begin to pray, imagining ourselves as babies. If you know how old you were when you began to walk, picture yourself at that age. Do you remember or are there photos of your house, yard, living room? Imagine your baby self pulling yourself up on a chair. Let yourself see that chair in technicolor. How big it is! You want to take a step. You are afraid. Your little legs wobble. You clutch the chair. A slight noise. God, your true Father (or your true Mother), has just entered your living room. God's face splits into a big grin. God knows you want to walk. Look at God smiling at you while hearing God speak these words (Hos 11:1, 3–4) directly to you.

> "When Israel was a baby, how I loved them!
> . . . It was I who taught my baby to walk, I who took them in my arms. . . . I led them with bonds of love. I lifted them, my little child, to my cheek, I bent down to feed them."

How do these words make you feel? Do you believe God loves baby-you? Picture God lifting you, nestling you against the very cheek of God, curving an arm to support your head as God gives your baby-self some warm, sweet milk. Rest. Feel. Trust.

> Like a weaned child on its mother's lap,
>   so is my spirit within me.
> My heart is longing for your peace,
>   so very close to you, my God (Ps 131).

When you get restless on God's "lap," return in memory/imagination to your living room, your struggle to pull yourself upright. God is still smiling. Now

God comes closer, ready to teach you to walk. How? You have to take a step away from that chair. God holds open welcoming arms. You wobble, you let go, you take one step. A second step. Your arms wave. A third step. Plop! What does God do?

Pause and talk over with God how you feel—about you, your baby-self, your trying to come closer to God, your falling plop on your seat. Tell God how you feel about God's smile, cheek, arms, encouragement. Now listen as God responds to you.

This is just one example of letting God's devotion to us (*hesed* and *'emet*) become very concrete. We encourage you to take the psalms and look for praise of, trust in God's *hesed* and *'emet*. Translations differ, so look for combinations like these: everlasting is God's love, God's mercy endures forever, God's kindness lasts forever, constant love and loyalty, faithful kindness, etc. Becoming aware of our woundedness, acknowledging God's desire to heal, or at least praying to trust a God whose name is faithful, extravagant, abundant, unconditional love is our first step toward healing.

Step Two: Discipleship

2. Step Two: Discipleship

Step two, in and toward grace: **Being willing to discard old remedies and "dirty bandages."**

Discipleship to most folks conjures up the image of the solitary Christian shouldering a heavy personal cross, head bowed, trying to follow the bloody footprints of Jesus to Calvary. Yet discipleship can be a joyful, hope-filled experience. John's gospel tells us so. Nowhere does the fourth gospel urge us to take up our cross and follow, but rather to open our eyes, ears, hearts and learn. *Discipulus/a* in Latin is a learner, a student. In this next step toward healing we will be learning, probably relearning. We will, making God's word our home, be deepening our discipleship, our learning from the Spirit of Truth. As Jesus promises his disciples the Spirit, he says: "No longer do I call you servants but friends, for I have made known to you all that I have learned from the Father" (Jn 15:15). Jesus speaks that good news to you. Hopefully it will give you the courage to relearn.

Take a moment to let this word sink in. Tell Jesus how you feel.

In this chapter you will be invited to look at some old, familiar ways and patterns which you and members of your

21

family may have developed to deal with the wounds created by the alcoholism of your parent(s). You will also be asked to re-examine some familiar images of God and some ingrained understandings of what it means to be human and to be spiritual. You can decide whether or not these patterns, images of God, and concepts still work for you. Hopefully, you will choose to let go of what doesn't work, or what doesn't lead you to truth and freedom. Be gentle with yourself though. These patterns and images did not develop overnight. Some of them will require more than just willingness to change. Old habits need new habits for replacement.

Defenses

All of us as we develop acquire certain defenses to protect ourselves against pain and responsibility. A number served us well at an earlier time of our development. As we get older, however, these defenses get in the way of mature and healthy decision-making and realistic responsibility. As we analyze a few defenses, take some time with each one, asking the Lord for light, for strategies, for courage to change.

Denial

The granddaddy of the alcoholic defenses is *denial*—a refusal to admit the reality which is there. We may deny our own drinking patterns, just as we may have denied patterns of a parent. An alcoholic has trouble seeing the damaging dimensions of his/her addiction. In the same way very often an ACOA has difficulty acknowledging being the child of an alcoholic. "My father wasn't really that bad, not like _____'s father." It is denial which motivates co-dependent parents to cover up for the drinking ones, calling in sick for them at work, defending their behavior to the children. Sometimes guilt ("It's my fault my spouse [my parent] drinks") makes denial necessary. It is denial which motivates the hope that if "we don't talk about it out loud, maybe it'll go away." Denial permeates so much of ACOA life that we need daily, even more frequent prayer, for the Spirit of truth.

Repression

Repression is a defense, a pushing of painful awareness out of consciousness. Allowing old wounds to fester, this defense can have very problematic consequences because our behavior and choices are governed by some old hurts which we don't even remember. Very often ACOA have a hard time remembering specific things about childhood. Painful memories have been repressed, yet inspire/govern/shape current behaviors.

The brother of a woman ACOA, in a family therapy session called because both parents were seeking treatment, told the family how he remembered a dark day in their teenage history. The woman's idolized (co-dependent) father, in defending the alcoholic mother from the girl's normal teenage sassiness (a sassiness undoubtedly but repressedly poisoned with her helpless fury at the drinking mother), slapped his daughter to the ground. Her brother's ability to remember this traumatic incident startled her, and then brought deep relief. She gradually became aware that the rupture of trust in her father was so great that it had subconsciously affected her subsequent relationship with the God she called Father. God was very important to this woman, yet she always waited for the "shoe to drop," for God "to get" her. Ninety-eight percent of the time she was sure of God's care for her but she waited and worried about a sudden display of God's wrath. Working with the memory, however, is gradually healing her fear of God.

Projection

Projection means attributing our own painful or hateful feelings to another or shifting responsibility for action. "My grandmother couldn't stand it when mother was drinking. She would get very angry." If we can't own our anger comfortably, we can project it onto Grandma. This kind of blaming is constant in the alcoholic home which makes it difficult for anyone to admit failure, wrong-doing, responsibility. ACOA can carry this defense into their own new families. Sometimes God gets blamed.

Reaction-Formation

Very often, because emotions such as anger or fear or hatred are so painful, a young person will develop the defense of *reaction-formation* or *reversal*. To protect ourselves against our terrible neediness or dependency we become super-independent: "I don't need anyone." Or we fence in our anger by becoming a super-nurturer and "kill" people with kindness. In other words, we will do in grand style the opposite of what we feel. Sometimes this leads ACOA to swear off all alcohol or even marriage; sometimes this leads them to become really fine parents, making amends in their own families for what they suffered growing up. The latter, however, tend to have made a free choice.

Fantasy

The only way for many a child of an alcoholic to escape suffering was withdrawal into *fantasy* where we could create our own safe world in our heads. Fantasy is good and useful both for escape and for rehearsal for real-life situations. It becomes dangerous when it serves as substitute for both the ordinary and the gourmet fare of reality. Especially in the area of relationships fantasy does not serve us well as adults because it keeps us from enjoying the ordinariness and limitations that are part of every relationship.

> Take a few minutes now. Relax and ask the Spirit of Truth to show you which of these defenses might be yours. Jot down in your journal a few examples of how you use them. Ask the Spirit to let you remember incidents from your childhood when these defenses served you. First, allow yourself to feel grateful for their service. Then, ask to let go, at least a tiny bit, of the defense right now. Write or draw symbols of your memories in your journal.

Crooked Thinking

Besides defenses which we may no longer need, "crooked thinking" may have helped us survive in the past but now may be crippling us. Practitioners such as David Burns, M.D. have identified this cognitive disorder as underlying, even creating depression and guilt.

First, we realize that our emotions are determined by how we perceive and think about reality. For example: I am riding on an interstate highway, busy talking to the driver. I cannot see the car that is careening toward us, crazily weaving. The car shoots past us and the driver tells me it was a close call. Because I didn't see what was happening my heart is not pounding wildly, my palms are not sweating like the driver's. With absolutely the same reality and danger, what changes the subjective feeling and experience is the perception. We will look at a few common cognitive distortions that we may have acquired, and we will consider some of their ramifications.

All or Nothing Thinking

Events, people, situations are all good or all bad, we mistakenly think. "Crooked thinking" at one level keeps life simple. It is a child's way of looking at reality. Where it becomes harmful in grown-up life is that it fosters perfectionism and intolerance of the raggedy ambiguity that is part of the human situation. For example, our alcoholic parent had a disease. Yet we may have spent a lifetime perceiving the alcoholic as all bad and the co-dependent, long-suffering parent as all good.

Catastrophizing

Assuming some awful outcome to a situation, we thus generate unnecessary internal anxiety. One ACOA tells the story of learning that kind of thinking as a child—how to "worry real good." Even before she knew that her dad had a drinking problem she used to watch her mother anguish at the slightest delay in his returning home. Mother always assumed that something awful, even fatal, had happened. Now as an ACOA she worries when worry is not called for. Instead of looking at the many rational reasons that an expected person is late—heavy traffic; delay at the office; stopping for an errand—she, like her mother, still assumes the worst.

Personalization

This is a favorite ACOA distortion and burden. Somehow if someone we care about is sad/mad/drinking it must be our fault. This terrible burden of a power we don't have is often felt by children in alcoholic families. If only I were smarter/ prettier/better behaved, Daddy, Mother wouldn't need to drink. The reality is that we cannot create feelings let alone a disease in another person. Of course, we have an impact on one another, but how we feel is more our own responsibility and response-ability than what someone else does to us. If someone we love is mad or sad there may be a million different reasons besides our "omnipotence" which has created the other's feeling.

Shoulds

Another type of cognitive distortion is the use of "should" and "ought" statements to keep oneself motivated. If we "should" ourselves we probably feel a great deal of pressure. Nothing is good enough. If our shoulds are directed at ourselves we experience guilt at not being able to live up to all our shoulds and oughts. (Notice the "all" in that last sentence!) If, on the other hand, we expect that others "should . . . " or "ought to . . . " we probably feel anger and resentment at their failures.

There are other forms of cognitive distortion such as using a *mental filter* to pick out and dwell on a negative detail so that our vision of reality gets clouded. Since all of these habits of crooked thinking are automatic it is helpful to:

a. be able to identify our "favorite" habit of crooked thinking;

b. be aware of the feeling that it produces in us, whether sadness, guilt, anger, fear, hatred, etc.;

c. be able to substitute a rational response for our distorted response.

Take some time now to try to identify patterns of automatic crooked thinking that you might use. One way to change these habits is to take some journaling time each day to:

    a. Pray, asking for the Spirit of Truth to guide you. Wait to see what bubbles up into consciousness.

    b. Write down the situation or event that bothers you or creates a negative feeling.

    c. Try to specify the negative feelings that were created such as anxiety, sadness, fear, anger.

    d. See if there are any automatic negative thoughts, for example, "I am a bad person" which is overgeneralization.

    e. Ask yourself if you *really* believe this. Then ask God if God believes this of you. Listen for God's response (and keep listening all through the day).

    f. Write down a more rational response, for example: "Sometimes I make mistakes but I also do many good things." Then name some. Check out your statements with God.

This technique is amazingly simple but very effective. If you want to learn more about it treat yourself to David Burns' book, *Feeling Good: The New Mood Therapy.*

The two "bandages" of defenses and crooked thinking which we have looked at so far are *intra*personal rather than *inter*personal. Because a family is a *system,* however dysfunctional or chaotic, there are a number of *inter*personal "bandages" that alcoholic families use. We will look at three of them here: roles; rules; and communication patterns.

Roles

A great deal has been written about ACOA roles in family systems. Claudia Black identifies the following:

The *Responsible Child:* adept at organizing, planning, getting things done. The "little adult" who managed the home and "covered" for the dysfunctional parent. Often an oldest child who ends up with responsibility for the care and protection of the little ones.

The *Placating Child:* the caretaker who watches out for everyone's emotional life. This is the child who tries to buffer the pain for the other children, giving great energy and empathy to the task of making others feel better—often at the expense of taking time to be a child him/herself. Sometimes a fun provoking, all the while denying the pain, family mascot.

The *Adjusting Child:* opts for peace at any price. He or she won't rock the boat or try to change anything. Such children go along as best they can using whatever emotional or physical disengagement is necessary to survive. The "lost child" is another name for this often depressed and withdrawn ACOA.

The *Acting Out Child:* externalizes the anger that exists in the family system. He/she acts out the chaos and confusion in the family in ways which draw negative attention. Even negative attention is more desirable than none at all.

Usually adults carry the behaviors of these roles into adult life and very often, although we have a "preferred" role, we can identify with more than one. The following is a lengthy exercise. You may want to use it over several days. Remember, healing is a lifelong process.

> Did you identify with any of these roles? They served you as a child. Thank God for their service. How do they still serve you?

> Breathe deeply. Let the Spirit of Truth well up from deep within you. Let the Spirit recall some incidents in which these roles let you survive. Be grateful.

Now ask the Spirit to light up the unfree aspects of these roles, unfreedoms that chain you. Tell the Spirit what you want to let go of. Breathe in the Spirit, breathe out the unfreedom.

"When I was a child I spoke and thought and acted like a child . . . " (1 Cor 13:10). In alcoholic families it's hard to be a child. Remember the gospel image of Jesus playing with and blessing the little children (Mt 19:13–15). Now hear Jesus inviting you to let your inner child come out and play. Picture the child who lives in you: clothes, hair color and style, body size, facial expression. Watch your child, watch your self, play . . . alone. Suddenly, Jesus comes strolling down your street and sits on your porch (swing, curbstone, front step). He opens his arms and smiles. What does your child do? Pause and watch.

"Let the little children come to me." Your dirty sneakers are messing up his clothes and still he smiles as you scramble up onto his lap. How does it feel for your baby self, your toddler self, your young self to be surrounded by his arms, his smile? Talk over *all* your feelings with him. Even if you feel like squirming down now, don't be afraid to tell him so.

Let your inner child tell Jesus all about your role in the family.

Listen to him say to the responsible child: "Come to me. You are so burdened. I will give you rest (Mt 11:28–30). Don't worry about what they will eat or what they will wear (Mt 6:25–33). Leave that to God. You just come to me."

Listen to Jesus say to the placating child: "Don't worry. I'll make peace (Eph 2:16). You can rest. I will bear your burdens day after day" (Ps 68:19).

Listen to the good shepherd say to the adjusting or lost child: "If you are hurt, I'll bandage you. If you are lost, I'll find you. If you are sick, I'll strengthen you. And when you are strong and healthy, I will set you out to play" (Ez 34:15–16).

Listen to the friend of sinners say to the acting out child: "Let's have a big party because you whom I have loved so dearly are coming home again" (Lk 15:23–24).

Rules

Most alcoholic families are characterized by inconsistency of rules, limits, discipline. Even if rules were unambiguous and clearly defined in the family, they probably were not consistently followed with the exception of the cardinal rule: "Keep the family secret." Children imbibed the most important, though perhaps unspoken rule not to hang out the dirty laundry of alcoholism in public.

Very often in such families the rules are not spelled out and become the focus of confusion because everyone assumes that everyone else knows what is expected. "Old" rules never get revised or updated. Unwritten, unspoken rules are often the most powerful, curtailing or distorting the freedom each person has to speak about what he/she feels, thinks, sees, hears, smells, etc. Don't talk, don't feel, and, because so much is distorted, don't trust—these are the key rules in the alcoholic family.

> With the Spirit of Truth, reflect on the family rules when you were a child. Ask the Lord to help you remember.
>   a. Were there any clear rules spelled out? For example, "If you must fight, no punching."
>   b. Did these work? (At least some of the time.)
>   c. How free were you to comment on
> what you felt . . .
> what you saw . . .
> what you thought . . .
> what you smelled . . . (heard, tasted, touched)
>   d. What were the unspeakable topics?

Research indicates that very often ACOA have experienced physical or sexual abuse as children. These often continue to be secret subjects for ACOA. Sexual ambiguity, silence about sex, and negative attitudes toward marriage may still burden ACOA, whether the abuse was overt or covert.

For example, in a healing of memories session an ACOA remembered how carefully, reverently and scientifically her mother spelled out the "facts of life" for her as a girl. Yet sexual activity, even feeling or phantasizing, set off almost suicide-provoking guilt in the unmarried ACOA. As she asked God for healing of an unhealthy sexual guilt, suddenly a memory rose up. Her sexual education had been delivered when she was nine. At age five, however, she had persuaded a neighbor boy to let her have a look at him. As an adult, her head told her that little children's investigations are normal, not sinful. Her heart was still plagued by guilt until the memory arose, a memory of the boy's mother storming into her living room and telling her (quite sober) mother of the incident. The mother hauled her five year old from under the table where she was hiding, pulled the girl's pants down in front of the neighbor, and walloped her rear end. Thus, four years later when Mom insisted how beautiful sex was, the child's wounded seat and wounded pride won out over her intellectual appreciation of sex.

Is there an incongruity like that in your life, a split between your knowledge and your feelings? Do you feel helpless before your guilt or your fear or your anger or your sexual desires or your hatred or your depression? If so, try to feel those feelings. The Spirit deep within us is putting our "unutterable groanings into words" (Rom 8:26). Ask the Spirit to reach into your memory. Ask for a memory to surface. Let it appear in all its concrete detail, including your feelings. Then invite Jesus into the scene.

The ACOA who had been curious about the neighbor boy, in her prayer as an adult, saw Jesus push open her front door, move into the living room, and ask the two mothers to stand aside. Taking the five year old on his lap, he stroked her hair and asked her what she had been doing. Jesus praised her desire to know things and explained that her Mom was very frightened by her own sexuality and was threatened by the neighbor's upset. The ACOA's compulsive sexual acting out began to wither away.

If you do not know Jesus too well, still he can show you through your prayer what and how he loves and hopes and heals. We recommend slowly reading through the gospels, first Mark's and then Luke's, always asking to know him more really, more deeply.

Communication

Another "bandage" which may have covered up and over pain in your family is the dysfunctional patterns of communication which might have existed in your home. Virginia Satir who has spent most of her professional life observing and working with families in distress has identified some patterns of communication which people use under stress. With these patterns they try to restore feelings of self-esteem which are under attack. They are a kind of defense which includes placating, blaming, computing, and distracting.

Many elements of communication may have gone awry in our alcoholic families. Communication is about sending and receiving messages. Most of the time both the sender and receiver are invested in the clarity of the message. Each of us brings to our communication our bodies, our senses, our brains, our history and our expectations. If we focus only on the words that are spoken, we underestimate the power of other factors.

Reflect on the power of visual cues and past experience in communication. Have you ever met someone who, without having spoken a word, reminds you of someone about whom you have strong positive or negative feeling? This person of the past predisposes you to listen to the present person in a certain way. Reflect also how body impacts communication. The anger expressed by a large person is often experienced more forcefully than anger expressed by someone diminutive, although there might not be much difference in decibel level.

When we feel threatened we often slip into a communication style in which the words (verbal content) and our body communications (body posture, facial expression, breathing, voice tone, etc.) do not deliver the same message. Satir has identified several common patterns of these double level communications. We usually revert to them when we feel threatened or worried about hurting someone or worried about their retaliation or rejection.

Have you ever experienced someone's telling you very bad news with a smile on his/her face? How did this make you feel? How did you respond? For example, we may hear a friend's words: "The doctor has discovered a hard mass in my breast" (potential bad news). Yet she communicates non-verbally by smiling with twinkling eyes ("Don't worry about me. I don't want to impose this on you"). As the receiver of this message, we may in our confusion respond only to one level of this message. The sender is disappointed; she too is confused.

Satir has identified some common communication patterns that we use to try to protect ourselves when threatened. See if any of these "fit" what you learned to do as a child or observed in your parents. Remember that each of these styles served to protect you against the threat of rejection, abandonment, feeling worthless, etc.

Placate—try to keep the other person from getting angry;

Blame—try to get the other person to see you as strong and in charge;

Compute—try to be so super-reasonable that you rationalize and minimize the threat you are feeling;

Distract—try to pretend the threat is not there, keeping the others entertained and distracted.

Take a few minutes now to think about each of these styles. It's helpful to exaggerate each of the styles with your whole body involved. Let your body assume an exaggerated posture of each of the styles so your whole self can really get into the feeling. If you are using this book in a group you might get different members to assume different styles and have a conversation.

For example, the *placater,* bowing or kneeling, tries to please, to agree, to ingratiate: "Yes, your majesty. No, your majesty. Give me a kick if it please your majesty." This bodily posture externally symbolizes the interior attitude. Psychologically, the placater is always on his/her knees, supplicating, worthless, begging, helpless. Sometimes this keeps the family somewhat smooth but the cost in self-esteem is very high. Often the placater feels progressively more depressed in this helpless, victimized position.

On the other hand, the *blamer* makes his/her mistakes with authority. Very often he/she projects his own littleness and limitations and tries to bolster feelings of self-worth by appearing strong and authoritarian and right. Again, let your body act out the role. How does it feel? Is it you? Does it release anything within you?

Very often blamers and placaters are drawn to one another. Archie and Edith Bunker portray these styles splendidly in *All in the Family*—Archie bellowing, blaming, blowing self-righteously and Edith scurrying around wringing her hands, apologizing for being alive.

The *computer* style of communication appears very correct, reasonable. Any show of feeling is taboo. The body language is stiff, rigid, detached. Have you ever been spoken to with icy cold, steely anger? Then, when you ask the person if he/she is feeling angry, you are shut down by his/her vigorous denial. If your favorite style of communication when feeling threatened is to shut off feelings and move into your head and use four syllable words to protect yourself, then you probably use the computer role.

The *distracter* on the other hand pretends to ignore the threat. To behave as though it isn't there may make the threat go away. Very often this communication style is the one adopted by the family mascot. It doesn't really matter what words we use to distract or entertain. If our insides feel like a top spinning out of control, it is because we feel as though our world is spinning out of control and if we can talk faster and funnier *away from* the real threat, then somehow the sum of two disequilibria will equal harmony.

Later on we will reflect on some of the dimensions of straightforward communication or what Satir describes as *leveling,* but for now try to identify the pattern that you slip into when you feel threatened. More than likely it is a pattern you learned as a child and one that worked (works) for you even though it has a price tag. As with other coping strategies mentioned in this chapter be grateful for how your communication pattern has served you, helping you to survive through your most threatened, helpless times. Then ask for the Spirit's gift of openness to the risks of level communication.

Word of God, we come in our confusions, asking you to open us up for your straightforward, growth-producing word. We hear your good news according to Isaiah:

"Come, you who are so hungry. Why work so hard and still not have bread? All you who are parched with thirst, come to living waters. For while your ways are not my ways, says the Lord, yet I will send my Word to you. Like rain and snow it will penetrate the earth of you and bring forth much fruit. My Word shall do in you all I sent it to do . . . and I will make a new covenant with you, to love you forever" (From Is 55).

Images of God

Jesus continues to make God known (Jn 1:18), and indeed knowing God *is* eternal life right now (Jn 17:3). All that anyone in any century has ever said about God falls short of the mystery of who God is. We use images of God, analogies for God, describe the activity of God, and yet there is more to learn. Because "definition" means to put limits on, we can never define God. Because God is mystery, God is infinitely knowable.

> Holy Spirit, we ask you to show us more deeply, more truly who God is. We want that abundant life of knowing God. We want to be more fully disciples, learners of our God. Help us to hold all our images and analogies lightly, no matter how precious or once nourishing. Our heads tell us God is more than mother or father, shepherd or savior, lover or lord. Help our hearts to learn how much more God is, and how much more God is for us.

If only our images of God were as positive as those in the prayer above! Unfortunately because *the* privileged image of God in the Judaeo-Christian tradition is Father, most ACOA are wary of God, afraid of being betrayed by God, just as they once felt helpless, betrayed, brutalized by their alcoholic fathers. ACOA with drinking fathers easily transfer their rage, need for approval, good works, fear, guilt, etc., to God the Father. For feminists to insist that we call God Mother does not alleviate the problem. Some ACOA had alcoholic mothers.

And all ACOA were betrayed by the co-dependency of even the non-alcoholic parent. The co-dependent parent gave a disproportionate amount of attention to the spouse when the alcoholic was drinking, and the children felt neglected. When the alcoholic was not drinking the co-dependent spouse was full of love and encouragement for the alcoholic, an attention for which the children hungered. Either way, alcohol was central in the family, actually controlled the family.

God is certainly *like* a good father but so much more good than any father we have ever known. God is *like* a good mother but so much more tender than any mother we have ever known. We don't usually know shepherds, shields, or fortresses, so it is easier to see how such titles merely image God. Perhaps parental images, and they are only images, analogies, will have to be discarded.

Don't be afraid. God realized that we were not getting an adequate picture of who God really is, though hundreds of authors, prophets, mystics, "friends of God" tried to image God for us in the pages of the Jewish scriptures. As the author of the Letter to the Hebrews phrased it: in so many and various ways God tried to communicate with us, but finally in these days, God sent a Son (Heb 1:1). The image of God *par excellence* is Jesus.

In former days, both in the history of the world and in our own personal salvation history, God expressed love for us as a covenant-maker; God and we bound ourselves to each other by the Jewish law. In these days God expresses who God is as Jesus, bound to us by "grace and truth," translations from those Hebrew concepts *hesed* and *'emet*.

Now the law came through Moses, but grace and truth have come to us through Jesus Christ (Jn 1:17).

In Jesus, God has come very, very close. If we want to know God, we need only look at Jesus. If we want to see God's *hesed* and *'emet* in the flesh (Jn 1:14) we pay attention to Jesus. "Whoever sees me, Philip, sees the Father" (Jn 14:9), sees God.

If we want to know what God wants, we look to see what Jesus wants. Jesus wants us to be abundantly alive (Jn 10:10). Jesus wants to heal, to open our eyes and ears. Jesus wants to straighten backs that have been bent, crippled for eighteen years (Lk 13:10–17), wants to stop the life-blood which has been draining out of us for twelve years (Mk 5:25–34), cast out the demons which have caused us to "cut ourselves with sharp rocks" out there in that "lonely place" (Mk 5:1–17). Jesus is not embarrassed if we need a big scene on center stage, if we need to sob and soak his feet in our desperation to be whole again (Lk 7:36–50). Jesus passionately wants our freedom. That is the will of God for us!

> Open your gospels to one of the gospel stories referenced in the last paragraph. Read the story slowly and out loud. Get inside the character of the one bent for years, bleeding for years, possessed by self-destructive demons or sobbing at Jesus' feet. Paint a very real scene in your imagination. Then feel the desperation, the longing of that gospel character. Feel your own desire for Jesus' hands to touch your pain and bring life. Speak to him with your feelings.

How can we be sure of God's desire to heal us, as we reflected on God's will in the first chapter? We look at Jesus' will, his passionate desire to heal, whole and free; at Jesus, the best image of God, and we see God's will for us.

> A two-part (two days or twenty days) exercise on what Jesus, imaging and embodying God, wants:

> (1) In Mark 1:40–45, a leper approaches Jesus ever so tentatively. "Master, if you want to, you can make me whole." Repeat the leper's line to Jesus over and

over again. Then, between repetitions, let a memory surface, for example, an abusive or humiliating scene with your parent. Hold the memory for a while, repeating, "Jesus, if you want to, you can make me whole." Then let another memory surface—until you begin to feel tired. You will, you know—sometimes you will be drained, exhausted, tearful. Come back another day Healing is a lifelong process.

(2) On another day, continue working with the healing of this leper. Notice that the leper doesn't really request anything of Jesus—just: "If you want to, you can make me whole." How frightening for a leper, such an outcast, a despised sinner (for illness was supposed to be punishment for sin), to make a direct request of anyone. How scary for an ACOA to make a direct request of anyone.

> "Master, if you want to, you can make me whole." Moved with anger, Jesus replied, "Of course I want to! Be made whole!"

Why is Jesus angry? In some manuscripts the phrase reads, "Moved with pity . . . " Why? Like us moderns, ancient translators may have well been frightened by anger. In the Stoic philosophy which prevailed in those times, it would have been wrong for Jesus to be angry. But he could have been—not angry so much at the leper but at those who convinced the man that he was beyond healing, that he shouldn't bother Jesus, that it was "God's holy will" that he should suffer so physically and psychologically. Jesus, with all the passion in him that hates pain, exclusion, labeling folks and families as sinful, insists: "Of course I want to!" His anger here puts power in his desire to heal. How could we doubt it? In fiery fury, he wants to heal us of the labels of leprosy which we ourselves and our families have carried, the isolation we have felt, the fear we have in making direct requests of him and/or of God and/or of anyone.

Hear him say to you again and again: "Of course I want to! Be made whole!" Let his word return to you often during the day.

Images of the Human Person, the Spiritual Person

Because *hesed* and *'emet,* that unconditional faithful love of God took flesh (Jn 1:14), we may have to re-examine, perhaps even throw away some old "bandages," attitudes about our humanity and our spirituality. First, let us pray—

A litany of thanksgiving from Romans 5:
Holy Spirit, God's own love poured out in our hearts
. . . thank you!

Holy Spirit, justifying us through faith . . . thank you!

Holy Spirit, saving us, reconciling us through Jesus
. . . thank you!

Holy Spirit, causing grace more to abound where once sin was in control . . . thank you!

From Romans 8:
Holy Spirit, setting us free from all condemnation
. . . thank you!

Holy Spirit, setting us free from the law . . . thank
you!

Holy Spirit, dwelling within our flesh, brimming
with life . . . thank you!

Holy Spirit, leading us from fear to friendship with
God . . . thank you!

Holy Spirit, promising us a share in Christ's splendor
as we now share Christ's suffering . . . thank you!

Holy Spirit, putting our pain in perspective . . .
thank you!

Holy Spirit, waiting within us, longing for God to set
our whole body free . . . thank you!

Holy Spirit, coming to the aid of our weakness . . .
thank you!

Holy Spirit, praying from deep within our human
flesh . . . thank you!

Holy Spirit, making all things work together for our
good . . . thank you!

Holy Spirit, transforming us gradually into the likeness of Jesus . . . thank you!

The most important shift in our understanding of our humanity and of our spirituality undoubtedly stems from the scriptural renewal of the last two decades. That the Word became flesh consecrates "all flesh, which sees the salvation of our God" (Lk 3:6). With our eyes fixed on Jesus (Heb 12:2), we have come to understand the importance of the incarnation. Flesh is not to be scorned or punished but is the very medium in which God's *hesed* and *'emet* became tangible for us. That shifts our spirituality, a many-meaning word which simply means our relationship with God. God comes to us in flesh, in all that is human. God not only penetrates our mind and will but our emotions, imaginations, perceptions, memories, words, dreams, actions.

Because Jesus is so human, relating to God in human, not angelic ways, we are freed from needing to be angels. We can dare to be real before a God who became so very real in Jesus. We have been rejected, abandoned, betrayed, neglected—just as Jesus was. God didn't rescue Jesus from all that pain but loved him through it into new, risen life. God, who takes the initiative in our relationship, is loving, saving, spiriting us right in the midst of our suffering. No need to clean up our lives before we "become spiritual." Even when (and if) we were God's enemies (Rom 5:10) God lavished the Spirit on us. The Spirit is the initiator of our spirituality. God's love poured into our hearts—first—makes us—second—capable of responding to God.

Our response to God we call prayer. As many ways as we respond, not just in times of formal prayer but hour by hour, is prayer. The Spirit continually prays within us. No need to work at our spiritual life, our prayer. It is all being done for us by the Spirit. "When we do not know how to pray the Spirit comes to the aid of our weakness" (Rom 8:26).

All the "unutterable groanings" of our lives, all that confusion, inconsistency, denial, escaping are shaped into prayer by the Spirit, God's love, poured out within us. No need to justify ourselves, prove ourselves, seek God's approval. No need to hide our weakness, our humanness, our sin. Grace is abounding and it is all God's gift, "not a reward for work done" (Eph 2:9).

> How immense the resources of God's grace, how great God's kindness. God, rich in mercy, because of such great love, brought us to life with Christ . . . . By God's grace we are saved, through trusting God. It is not our own doing . . . We are God's work of art (Eph 2:7–10).

Jesus is the best image of God. The Spirit is transforming us moment by moment into a more complete image of Christ. We are God's work of art. Spirit and flesh, we are created in God's likeness. To learn this, to trust this, is to be graced in abundance. To learn this is to be more truly a disciple.

Step Three: Conversion

3. Step Three: Conversion

Step three, in and toward grace: **Be willing to go into the pain to change.**

Philosopher Ernst Becker assesses two fundamental human desires: to be special and to surrender one's self. Psychologist Irving Yallom nuances the two: to be special and to be rescued. Theologian John Shea writes of the self-justifying heart and rejected heart. Spiritual director Brian McDermott points out "the falsely assertive and harmfully dependent ego." Authors of ACOA books name the roles as family hero and lost child.

No matter who we have been, who we are or what we want, conversion means that we will be changed, stripped, surrendered. The assertive will learn dependence, the rejected will be loved, the dependent will learn to stand straight. In the biblical Hebrew, conversion is *shub,* re-turn; in Greek it is *metanoia,* a change (*meta*) of mind (*noia*). In English conversion means literally a turning (version) with (con). We will all turn, we will all change. In this step toward healing we will be turning with. We are not alone in our pain of the past nor in the pain that conversion will cost. We are turning with— and the "with" means with Jesus. We are going to have a heart-to-heart talk with, a hurt-to-hurt dialogue with our very human brother Jesus. If our hearts and hurts are to be opened, then God too will open God's own heart, God's own hurts. If our hearts are to be laid bare, ready for transformation, conversion, then together with Jesus we will open God's heart to see what's there.

In this step in and toward grace, we will have to let the wound of our history be cleansed. Some of the old bandages and dead skin have hopefully begun to peel away. Now comes the astringent, the Spirit who seeps in deeply, helping us go right into the wound, through the pain. To delve into pain will be particularly difficult because we have spent so long covering up pain, denying our feelings, hiding out from conflict, pretending to have it all together (special, self-justifying, falsely assertive family hero), letting our fear cripple us (waiting to be rescued, rejected, harmfully dependent lost child). The Spirit is a careful, gentle, patient agent of cleansing and healing. Already deep within us from the time of our baptism, the Spirit has been working inner healing, and will not hurry us now. What we do is simply, more consciously feel the Spirit at work in our healing, trying to be as patient and gentle with ourselves as God is. Here is a story and exercise about God's patience embodied in Jesus:

> A woman bent for eighteen years feels Jesus' hands on her (Lk 13:10–17). Scrunched over, she, not by her own free choice, nonetheless is protecting her vital organs. (The shorthand of the gospel stories sometimes leads us to believe that Jesus' healing of the people in his life was instantaneous. Maybe not so.)

> Imagine that you have been bent for so many years (and you have been). How painful to change. How unprotected your vital organs will be, how exposed.

How frightening to trust yourself to Jesus. Feel the fright. Tell Jesus all about your fear.

Slowly, then, you straighten up. Imagine the pain in your atrophied muscles, the stretching of such weakened tendons, the new movement in your spine which almost rips you in two. How much more comfortable to hunch over again. How much more safe to keep looking at the world askew from your twisted but well defended view point.

Look at Jesus looking at you. He understands why you don't snap up, tall and straight. He watches your pain sweep over you, the pain in your spine, the pain in your spirit. His face is twisted like yours in agony. He is feeling your fear of change, your terror at turning so late in life to freedom and health. He can do no more. Still, he encourages you, nods, stretches out his hands. The acceptance of your healing begun, however, is your choice now.

And the good news? Even if you scrunch back up in your helpless, hopeless position, Jesus is not going to go away. He will not abandon you but will return in season and out of season, in times of prayer and in times of sin, in chance meetings with old friends or in planned meetings with a therapist, in a time of new pain or new peace to invite you again to let his strong hands straighten you into wholeness. Thank him in advance for the healing he offers and which one day you will accept. Share all your feelings with him.

Share all your feelings with him. Feelings are some of our most "vital parts," those emotions which we have kept covered for so long, bending, twisting them to keep our view of the world, others and God slightly off balance. Once we were told that a spiritual person needed to become angelic, controlling and "mortifying" the body, especially feelings. The biblical renewal, however, has opened up for us the quite emotional spiritual journeys of women and men in both Old and New Testaments. Their very emotions were ways of relating to God. In this step in and toward grace, we will focus on the whole range of feelings and emotions. Many ACOA have learned that the most manageable way to deal with feelings is to deny or repress them, keeping them as far away as possible from awareness. Perhaps quite adept at tears, joy, or compassion, we often deny anger, fear or hate. There is much evidence, however, that feelings which are not available to awareness have a great deal of power. To name a feeling gives us a better chance to tame it, to channel it, and not be controlled by it.

There are many ways to identify the probable feeling experiences of the child of an alcoholic. Inconsistent parenting is an experience of loss, sometimes of abandonment. One ACOA relates: "I remember vividly as a child sitting out in the cold car while Dad was in the bar. Lots of times Mom would go in with him. I guess she figured he wouldn't drink as much if she went in with him. I think my brother and sister were very scared too but we never talked about it. Just got colder and colder." These children were probably experiencing fear, fear of abandonment, sadness, anger. Not only were their bodies chillingly numbed by this wait in the car but their feelings were numbed. Children experience time as more elongated than adults. An hour can stretch endlessly, even if the car isn't cold.

Another ACOA remembers: "I must have been four or five. Daddy took me with him while he went to the barber shop. This was years before I learned to hate the barber shop because it was next to the bar. It seemed like forever that he was gone and I knew with a frightening kind of certainty that I have seldom since experienced that he was gone forever and wasn't coming back. I was too little to realize that he probably hadn't forgotten what the car looked like or where he had parked it in our sleepy little town. My panic was absolute and I never let myself be that vulnerable to feelings again until I was an adult in therapy." This ACOA's panic and fear of abandonment was undoubtedly sharpened by the fact that her mother had died when she was an infant. She continues to struggle with feelings of vulnerability to abandonment but at least being able to claim and name the feeling has allowed her to tame it.

To become more aware of feelings it is helpful to use your safe place and your journal to express these feelings. To feel is not sinful but is an expression of God's gifts to you: your emotions. Hopefully your partners in friendship, ACOA group or therapy can be with you in this. You will probably experience that your journey into the wound of your past, integrating painful feelings and emotions, also frees you and makes you more available to emotions of joy and love. Be patient with yourself though. God is.

First of all, what are some of your own feelings *about* feelings? What were some of the messages which you received about feelings when you were growing up? Were you taught implicitly or explicitly that feelings are not important, that some feelings are good and others are bad?

Take some time to reflect on your own "feeling history" of:
- fear
- surprise
- sadness
- anger

- exhilaration
- joy

Ask the Spirit to help you remember, over several days, concrete incidents of these emotions in your personal salvation history.

Emotions are body/spirit phenomena. They have a physiological as well as a psychological component. Therefore it is impossible not to feel even if we have learned to repress or deny feelings. Swallowed anger can burn a hole in stomach linings or cause headaches or asthma. Paradoxically, it is impossible not to express feelings, even when we can't name what the feeling is. Remember some non-verbal ways you have expressed anger: pouting, withdrawing, "forgetting," stomping.

A useful step in identifying feelings is to claim them as our own. To name our anger and to claim it as our feeling, to take responsibility for it instead of blaming someone else, is more truthful, more free, and thus more in tune with the Spirit of Truth. "I feel angry" instead of "You make me mad" is more true. Others do not cause us to feel, although another person can stimulate a feeling in us.

In our families in which blaming, anger, even violence erupted, most of us learned ways to avoid taking responsibility for our emotions. Instead of using "I" statements about our feelings we may have labeled, questioned or blamed. "I" statements, however, communicate more clearly. For example, LABELING: Instead of labeling, "You are arrogant," we can learn to say, "I feel furious." "That jerk!" when someone acts crudely could be expressed "I feel embarrassed." QUESTIONS: The driver may not slow down if we ask: "Is it really safe to drive this fast?" Yet it is more risky (and honest) to state, "I feel scared." BLAMING: "I feel unloved" underlies the angry, pouting "You don't give a damn about me."

Call on the Spirit of Truth. Ask the Spirit to show you just one feeling you felt today or yesterday. Practice using an "I" statement about it.

Begin another practice. Ask the Spirit each day to put your "inarticulate groanings" (Rom 8:26) into words so that you can be aware of, understand, claim as your own, and appreciate your emotions. Say to the Spirit each time you become aware of a feeling: "I feel . . ."

Anger deserves special attention because it is a powerful emotion which many of us were encouraged to stifle. Anger is a subjective emotion. There are a million irritants in everyday life which can make us feel angry. Being caught in traffic, getting blamed for someone else's mistake, being hounded by an over-eager salesperson are sample events that may make one person angry and leave another quite calm. We feel anger when we perceive a threat to our physical or emotional well-being or when we are frustrated trying to satisfy a need which we perceive as important.

One of the critical internal changes that ACOA are called to is a reassessment of how we perceive the threats and frustrations which precipitate anger inside us. The angry-making potential of our perception comes from two sources. First, how dangerous is this threat to me? And then, do I have the resources to deal with this threat? Very often as adults we don't take the time to reassess either the threat to our well-being or our resources to deal with the threat. Carrying the scars of what was in reality very threatening to a child, we react as though we still have only a child's resources.

An ACOA tells the story of looking out the window as a little child to see if grandfather was walking in a straight line coming in from work. His staggering meant very drunk and

usually signaled uproar for the evening. Her impotence to pre-
vent Mommy from crying made her feel bad (later she could
name "bad" as anger and fear). The child pressured herself to
be super-good and not add even a jot to the family upset by
letting her fear and anger out. Not surprisingly as an adult, she
has a hard time expressing anger, swallowed over the years;
burdened by a too-responsible "nice-ness," she struggles with
depression.

To deal with anger, first we claim it. We try to name the
threat we are feeling or the needs which are being frustrated.
If we don't own our anger we will probably act it out without
even realizing that we are. The blatant slogan, "Don't get angry, get even," while shocking to "good" persons, may be
their own underlying attitude to being late, forgetting. This is
passive anger, one of the most difficult feelings to deal with,
partly because we are out of touch with our own anger, re-
pressing it until it leaks out in ways destructive to others—and
to ourselves.

Secondly we diagnose the threat, that is, reassess our perception. Is the other really that dangerous or really taking
something from us? This is a tricky step for ACOA because as
children our alcoholic parent(s) probably was in reality a
threat to either our physical or our emotional well-being.
"Would tonight be the night that Dad bursts into my bedroom
and beats me with his belt for a real or imagined offense?" an
ACOA remembers. "Is Mom (and all my adult women friends)
going to twist and violate the confidence I shared with her this
afternoon when she seemed so inviting of my trust?" another
ACOA asks. But do we now give to all adults the power to
harm us because once we experienced our parents erratically
using power over us? We cannot always just think our way out
of this painful generalization. The Spirit is within us, converting us. *Meta-noia* means changing our way of thinking.

We reassess too our adult resources right now. True, we

have scars but we also have strengths. Tell someone about these. Sharing helps. It is also helpful to develop ways to discharge some of our anger energy: exercising, pounding a pillow, twisting a towel, tearing up a nerf ball, growling. (Yes, growling!) But be sensitive to what helps *you*. Sometimes vigorous exercise parodoxically can produce more anger. Perhaps your concern is not expressing your anger but rather controlling your own expression of it. Try to be patient with where you are right now. The Spirit is working down deep with all your "inarticulate groanings." The last step—letting go of the anger so God can gift us with forgiveness—will weave through the rest of this book.

Every feeling which we have ever experienced, Jesus has felt. He is "like us in every way, except sin," that is (according to Jewish concepts of sin prevalent in those times), rebellion against God (Heb 4:15). Because "he has been tested like us in every way, we have a compassionate high priest" (Heb 2:17–18). Emotion is not sin. Literally it means a movement (motion) out of (e) ourselves. Emotions are God's gifts to us, to move us away from evil and threat, to move us toward the good and beautiful, to move us toward truth.

Having examined a whole range of human feelings, so many of which we may have repressed, we will now examine Jesus' human experience as best we can. Our chief tools will be the gospels and our own experience, for Hebrews (12:1–2) also tells us that Jesus has pioneered the way for us. Anything which we feel now, he has felt first, as our pioneer, like us in everything. What emotions did Jesus feel?

Ask the Spirit of Truth to teach you all you need to know about Jesus (Jn 14:26).

Then ask Jesus the following questions and wait quietly for some gospel scene to arise or some scene

which *could* have happened because Jesus is just
like us, our pioneer. In order to savor all that he
wants to share with you, we suggest that you take
only one of Jesus' emotions a day, or one per prayer
period. Ask him:

Jesus, when were you ever lonely?
Jesus, when were you afraid?
Jesus, when did you feel guilty?
Jesus, when did you feel tender?
Jesus, when did you hate?
Jesus, when did all seem hopeless?
Jesus, when were you sad?
Jesus, when did you feel strange, "out of it"? Weird?
Jesus, when did you get annoyed?
Jesus, when did you get furious?
Jesus, when did you walk away from conflict?
Jesus, when did you feel overjoyed?
Jesus, when did you feel revenge?
Jesus, when did you feel empty?
Jesus, when did you feel jealous?
Jesus, when did you get depressed?
Jesus, when did you feel anxious?
Jesus, when did you feel sexually attracted?
Jesus, when did you feel helpless?
Jesus, when did feelings of violence arise in you?
Jesus, when did you ever panic?
Jesus, when did you feel grateful?
Jesus, when did your heart melt with love?

As Hebrews instructs, you have been keeping your
"eyes fixed on Jesus, our pioneer" (12:2).

Now return to the list of Jesus' emotions and share
with him, he who knows from the inside out what

every emotion feels like (the intensity, the fear of overdoing it, the release) when *you* have felt each of those emotions listed. How does Jesus respond as you remember each of these emotions in your life?

If no memory of your emotion arises, ask Jesus to show you, but then leave it alone. For example, maybe you haven't allowed yourself to feel jealousy yet. Perhaps violence frightens you because you're so lady-like, or tenderness repels you because you are so manly. Talk with Jesus about how you are stifling these bits of being human. You are not your jealousy, your violence, your tenderness, but they are parts of your personality, gifts of a creating God to be used for good. Jesus, it seems, could go into an emotion, feel it bodily right down to his bones, then choose to use it or to let it go. He was free to let his emotions give him the energy to move away from threat, through pain, into truth and love. Before we, however, can discern whether to use our emotion or let it go, we must feel, not deny any of them.

For example, because many ACOA have buried anger they are deeply afraid that were there one little crack allowed in the volcano that is within, the eruption could destroy all whom they love, and themselves. They are secretly addicted to this anger which feeds off their vitality and so they maintain strong, loyal ties to destructive people and situations. Instead of having the necessary freedom to discern whether a spouse, a parent, an institution (like this job or that parish) truly needs and/or deserves our devotion, we hang on long after the juice and joy have disappeared. This is not to advocate a quick-fix escape from painful situations. This is to advocate letting the Spirit gradually lead you into the deep wound of your buried anger which terrorizes you with its power. The Spirit is called *dynamis,* another word for power, energy, in the Greek of the New Testament. The Spirit's power can free and channel and guide your expressions of anger so that your fidelity, if that is the outcome of your search for truth, will be free and not an addiction to a martyr's role.

Finally, a caution about conversion. The martyr's role, the virtuous strong and silent role, the heroic and selfless role may all have to be converted. Usually we think of being converted from sin and guilt, but our goodness needs converting as well. Jesus told a story about two people who went up to the temple to pray (Lk 18:9–14). Not only did the sinner (the rejected, longing to be rescued, lost child) need God's mercy. Even more so, the good man who in his self-asserting virtue was blind to his dependence on God needed conversion. Both kinds of us can "go home justified," when we beg God to change our minds and hearts.

At this point, if you have not read and worked through Patty McConnell's book, *Adult Children of Alcoholics: A Workbook for Healing* (Harper and Row), we highly recommend that you do.

Step Four: Community

4. Step Four: Community

Step four, in and toward grace: **Expose the wound to light and air.**

To heal is an intransitive verb. We do not heal anyone, even ourselves. All we can do is prepare the wound for healing. Healing comes from within. It cannot be achieved, but if we expose the wound to healing elements: medicine, oil, light, air, "all things work together for good" (Rom 8:28). In this chapter we will look at the healing grace which comes to us mediated by those who love us and those whom we love, our community. We will review some techniques to communicate with these people more honestly. We will especially focus on Jesus who is called light and on the Spirit, the breath of God, who are working within us and within our relationships for our health.

This step in and toward grace, exposing the wound, cuts at the heart of one of the most pervasive pains in an alcoholic home: covering up. We don't talk about alcohol, about our fear, anger or guilt. We learn to lie and to deny so that often we are not even aware of our lying. We construct with words a false reality and prop up our unreal world with more lies which even we come to believe.

Some ACOA lie blatantly. One woman tells of her shame

that her father was the town drunk; away at college, she would assert: "My daddy is a college professor, respected in the county." ACOA report that sometimes, however, they lie even when there is no reason to, no threat, no shame. Or they say "I can't" do such and such when they mean, "I don't want to." Some bluster and exaggerate, some use pollyanna platitudes, some dig into untruth, laying excuse upon excuse. All need the light of Christ to shine in the darkness. This light defeats the "Father of lies," the devil of John's gospel.

Most ACOA don't particularly want to lie, but often their communication is distorted and does not function well, is "dysfunctional," and actually confuses those who try to listen and respond. Earlier we promised to discuss more fully what Virginia Satir describes as "leveling" in communication. Communication is basically a feed-back loop between two "poles," the sender and the receiver. As in radio communication, the message can get distorted or jammed either by the transmitter or by the receiver. In trying to communicate clearly it is important that all "levels" of signaling are congruent. Our verbal message needs to correspond to our non-verbal signals, and hopefully both of these will be congruent with our feelings. To say "I am hurting" with a smile confuses the signals and the response.

Dysfunctional communication styles are present in alcoholic families. Sometimes too we have assumptions that if there is intimacy between two people we don't need to state needs and feelings expressly. A common mistake is that two people who really care for each other can read each other's mind. "If he/she really loves me, I wouldn't need to ask. . . ." There is such vulnerability in asking clearly for what we want because it leaves us open to the risk of the other's saying "No." "Level" communication requires that we take responsibility for our needs and feelings and try to articulate these as clearly as possible.

There is a vulnerability about self-disclosure that is very real. On the continuum of conversational intimacy, however, the two most intimate forms of communication are (1) self-disclosure, and (2) feedback, which means responding to that self-disclosure of another by sharing feelings. The intimacy we long for calls for that risk of communicating clearly *and* with/ about our feelings as well as our ideas, projects etc.

Receiving communication is as important as speaking. Good listening was probably not modeled well in an alcoholic home. Healing can happen when another really listens, attends to us. Careful attending is communicated by eye contact, posture, reflecting what we have heard to the speaker. Good listening, focusing fully on the other, is a skill which needs to be cultivated with as much care as other communication skills.

Both speaking and listening need to happen with other persons and with God in order for healing to happen. Many ACOA are finding in the experience of ACOA groups the healing which occurs when we are able to speak about the dark places in which we have lived so long. Group therapy, whatever its focus, can be a very powerful means for healing in community. Realizing how universal are some painful experiences or shameful behaviors helps to heal isolation and guilt. The support and nurturance of being listened to and understood, the challenge of being stretched to leave the prisons of our childhoods, the chance to live even an hour a week in a "family" which corrects some earlier emotional damage are all immense benefits of a group experience. There we can learn both to expose some old wounds and to practice some new strategies of communication and behavior. We can gradually move toward clearer communication. We can learn to walk more in truth.

There are bits and pieces of all of us that "walk in darkness and the shadow of death." But the ACOA grew up in so much darkness that reality can be as distorted as shadows dancing on a wall. If we say we have no sin, no darkness, we lie, the author of John's First Epistle proclaims, but "if we live our lives in the light . . . we are in union with one another" (1 Jn 1:6–7). The good news is that the light shines in our darkest, dankest, most lonely spots within. Christ's healing light reaches into our innermost hideouts. "In your light we see light," the psalmist sings to God (Ps 36:9).

> Another translation of Psalm 36:9 is: "In your light, we are bathed in light." Imagine Jesus' hand, his glorified wounded hand, streaming light. Now he moves to touch you.

> Imagine his light-filled hand on your head, bathing your ideas, imagination, memory in his light. Then he moves to stroke your face; your face, bathed in light, relaxes its bitter scowl or its tense protectiveness or its sickly sweet smile.

> His hand drops gently on your shoulder and the burdens drop away. His light touches each of your organs, glands, nerves. He bathes your anger in light, your fear, your grief. His light penetrates your whole body, your whole consciousness. In his light, you and every deep dark, scary, lonely, lost part of you are bathed in light.

Not only will this light who is Christ bathe our hidden, guilty, frightened parts but it will put our worth, gifts, love into new perspective. We can never know ourselves in isolation, without the reflection of others. Our most significant others in our most impressionable years often fed back to us how insignificant, worthless, dumb, bad we were/are. That is simply not true, nor is it humility to maintain such low self-esteem. Jesus lights up all our gifts from God, thanks us for our love and service and goodness, accepts us, praises us, trusts us, honors us in ways our parents could not. "I would give whole worlds for you," God tells each of us through Isaiah. "You are worth more than all the nations to me" (43:3–5). And indeed, to prove God's love for each of us who have worked so hard to prove our love, God gave each of us Jesus, the Word, the light.

Jesus in turn gives us the Spirit. "I will not leave you orphans" (Jn 14:18). One of our worst fears is being abandoned. To heal that fear, Jesus gives us the Paraclete, sometimes called counselor, comforter. In the Jewish scriptures the Spirit was called the breath of God. In former days the Spirit "wrapped 'round" the heroes of Israel, but in our time the Spirit is deep within us. In former days the Spirit hovered over the chaos (Gen 1:2); in our time the Spirit deep within us hovers over our personal chaos and groans within our subconscious (Rom 8:26). The Spirit is the breath of God breathed deep into us, uniting us constantly to our God.

> Breathe deeply, slowly for a minute. Now imagine with each intake how you are breathing in God's Spirit. Breathe out fear. Breathe in the Spirit. Breathe out hostility. Breathe in the Spirit. Breathe out a specific hurt. Breathe in the Spirit. Breathe out a concrete sorrow. Breathe in the Spirit. Continue as long as you choose, trying to become more and more specific as you breathe out all that troubles you.

The Spirit deep within us puts our unutterable groanings into words which God can understand (Rom 8:26). The Spirit, healing us from within, can also straighten and clarify our groanings without, can guide our words, our communication with others, especially those we call community: our family,

both of origin and of our own creation; friends and co-work-
ers; therapists, pastors and spiritual directors. The Spirit is the
bond of our community, the life-force which holds us all together in the body of Christ. The Spirit, God's own love
poured out in our hearts (Rom 5:5), wants to un-confuse, in-
tensify and deepen our reception of love and our offering of
love. To expose ourselves to community, to receive unconditional, extravagant love from God/Jesus/Spirit/community,
is to be more and more healed both from within and from
without.

At this point you may want to participate in an ACOA
group in your neighborhood. You might also want to form a
group for faith-sharing, using the materials and exercises of
this book. The cardinal rule of faith-sharing is not to evaluate,
not to judge anyone's contribution, past experience, or present relationship with God—not to evaluate another's contribution but not to evaluate your own either. Our experience
indicates that if an ACOA is not given to swaggering and
boasting, most of us de-value our pain, our worth, our relationship with God. God works with and within each of us so
uniquely. In a faith-sharing group we are invited to marvel at
God's unique way with each of us. There are no right or wrong
comments in faith-sharing, no better or more mature ways to
let God heal us, grace us. All we can be, by opening our experience to the community and receiving each of theirs, is en-
riched.

The Word of God promises: "If you make my word your
home, you will be my disciple. You will know the truth and
the truth will set you free" (Jn 8:32). Secure in the Word of
God we can learn to expose more of ourselves in honest ways,
to "level," communicating more clearly and so strengthening
our relationships, both intimate and in community.

Step Five: Union

5. Step Five: Union

Step five, in and toward grace: **Let the wound be, let it rest and heal slowly from within.**

A wound is fascinating. We constantly check it for signs of healing, sometimes touching it till it begins to bleed again. In this process of healing, we can't probe too steadily lest we try to take healing into our own hands, rush it, and spoil the progress the Spirit has accomplished. So, in this step, we rest, taste the union with God which our brokenness has brought. "The Lord *is* close to the brokenhearted, to those crushed in spirit" (Ps 34:18).

The Spirit keeps us constantly united with God, crying, "Abba-Daddy-Mommy" (Rom 8:15); or crying, if parental images harm us, "Giver-Helper-Lover-Friend-Healer." The Spirit prays continually within us for our healing, when we sleep, through our dreams; when awake, through every thought, decision, action the Spirit prays—and heals. This union with God, God's gift to us, is accomplished, and we, we can rest.

God has said to us, "I will take the heavy burdens from your backs" (Ps 81:6). "God bears our burdens for us day after day" (Ps 68:19). We are invited to rest. Jesus reiterates the good news: relax. "Come to me, all you who are heavy burdened, and I will give you rest" (Mt 11:28–30).

71

This resting does not mean inactivity. It means receptivity. To remain open and receptive to God, God's ways, God's healing is difficult for the take-charge family heroes. To keep one's attention on God instead of on oneself is difficult for the lost children. To be quiet is difficult for the mascot.

Another name for this receptivity, this quiet alertness, waiting for God, is a contemplative attitude. In Psalm 81, God asks us to open up: "If only you would open your mouths I would feed you . . . with the finest wheat, the best of honey" (Ps 81:10, 16). How much God wants to lavish on us, Paul exclaims—not just all we need but "all that God has to give" (Rom 8:32).

What has God lavished on you lately? Take pen and paper and make a list. Don't write what you *should* feel grateful for but what, as you remember the person, event, situation in specific detail, really causes a *feeling* of being loved, lavished on.

ACOAs are deprived of so much that we can't believe anyone could ungrudgingly give to us, let alone lavish upon us. How difficult to trust!

Let's try to trust. We will enlist our bodies in this prayer. Often our bodies tell us through pain, tension, insomnia what our spirits can't bear. Our bodies now will prepare us to receive all God wants to give. Open your hands, palms up, spread out your arms, tilt back your head, open your mouth and beg God to feed you, not just the meat and potatoes of our daily bread but the finest delicacies, the honey of all that God has to give. In this receptive posture, tell God not only what you need but what you want.

It is not enough to rest and receive in times of prayer. In relationship too we need to take baby steps, asking others directly for what we need, accepting compliments with a simple thank you, spending a little money on ourselves. You know where your attitudes and behaviors are not free, not simple, not receptive. Attitudes which are closed, behaviors which are controlled and controlling, will gradually begin to yield as we take tiny steps of trust and receptivity, letting the Spirit direct our lives (Gal 5:25), trusting God's passionate desire to lavish on us all that God is.

Step Six: Forgiveness

6. Step Six: Forgiveness

Step six, in and toward grace: **Forgiveness of the wounding one(s) by becoming an instrument of healing.**

"No one will be blamed," assures Patty McConnell in *Adult Children of Alcoholics: A Workbook for Healing,* as she leads her readers through self-awareness exercises. No one is, in her book. Yet in our lives we may well be blaming our alcoholic parent, our co-dependent parent, our eldest sibling who didn't take charge or who left home (read: left me), our grandparents and ancestors who brought the disease into our bloodline. We may well be blaming God for putting us into this kind of family or putting the disease into our own bodies. Our heads may figure all kinds of ways to rationalize the blame. As once we defended our parents from blame we may think we have to defend God. God, however, invites us to give our heads a rest and use our bodies to express years, decades of blaming rage. God invites us to clench our fists and start to beat on God.

> Do just that. Clench your fists. Let all the pain of the past twenty or forty or sixty years flow right into those clenched fists. Let all the fury, violence, hatred, revenge of so many years energize those fists. Now

77

punch. Stand up and punch. Shout at God. Detail the loss, the grief, the anger. Beat your fists on God. God is big enough to take your rage. God won't die from your blows and your blame. God is not fragile, nor is God frightened by fury.

When you finish, rest quietly and pay attention to your responses. Tell God/Jesus/Spirit in more modulated tones just how you feel and what you want now.

Alcoholism is a disease. "The alcoholic is a good person who's controlled by an insidious disease," Patty McConnell writes. She asks us to draw the disease. In *Down All the Days*, novelist Christy Brown envisions his alcoholic father's burial. From out of his father's now physically dead brain crawls a huge, ugly, ferocious rat. Draw the disease, McConnell urges, and the healing behind that is to have us objectify the disease. Our fathers/mothers are not alcoholism. Our fathers/mothers are good persons who are

> . . . controlled by an insidious disease. Consumed by rage and guilt, the alcoholic withers, helpless and confused. On your journey to wholeness, try to separate the pathology from the person so that you may understand that the alcoholic in your life was, or is, ill. The disease has hurt the alcoholic as much as it has hurt you (McConnell, p. 120).

Understanding does not mean excusing, for that would be again to deny the pain, to get caught in unreality. To understand means to realize that the disease is evil; its effects in our lives were and are evil, damaging; its effects will linger through our entire lives. Nor will understanding and forgiveness come all at once. Insight and the desire to forgive will recur and recur. If the effects of growing up in an alcoholic home will linger all our lives, so will the grace of healing linger. Each time we understand more deeply, more fully, each time we forgive more freely, we are letting God who "began this good work in us bring it to completion" (Phil 1:6). We regress, close our minds, harden our hearts, steeling them against further forgiveness, but once we want healing, want to forgive, God will not give up on us—ever.

Jesus was attracted to the sick. "I come, not for the healthy who have no need of a doctor," he proclaims again and again, not only in word but in action. "I come for the sick." He calls sickness, sickness; demons, demons; sin, sin. He calls our parent(s) sick, not demons no matter how wild their words and weird their behavior, not sinners no matter how many sinful acts they committed while drinking. He comes not for all those healthy parents, wholesome families we envied so while growing up. He comes for my sick dad, my sick mom, my sick family, my sick self.

> Picture each member of your family in his/her situation now. Watch Jesus enter his/her house or apartment or hospital room or jail cell or . . . Each member of your family is sick whether he or she is drinking, whether your alcoholic parent died years ago. Each member of your family is wounded, sickened by at least one member's disease of alcoholism. Hear Jesus say to each member of your family, "I come for you . . . (John or Joe or Angie or . . .). Watch Jesus hold out both hands, streaming light from his glorified wounds, walk closer to your father (mother, brother, grandma . . .), tip both his hands over and rest them on the head of your sick family member. Watch the healing power of Jesus go out

from him (Mk 5:30) and into your relative. See your relative light up inside, begin to glow outside. Know and give thanks that Jesus is with each of your family members right now, healing.

During the weeks and months ahead whenever you make contact (letter, phone call, visit or just a thought), "send" Jesus to your sick relative. As you practice sending Jesus to heal the sick, he will gradually be healing you of grudges, hurts, hostilities, competitions, neglects, envies—all those wounds alcoholism brought to your family.

As you pay attention to Jesus, one day you will hear his invitation to forgive. Forgiveness of those who have damaged us, sometimes it seems irreparably, is not an action we can choose but is God's gift to give when God knows we are ready. That is why, in our last chapter, we asked you to foster an open, receptive attitude toward God's ways, God's gifts, and others' kindnesses to you. Open, receptive, alert to the Spirit moving in our own hearts, we will know the moment is right to receive God's gift of forgiveness.

Breathe in the Spirit of forgiveness. As you exhale, pray: Thank you for letting me forgive . . . (mom or grandpop or uncle Tony or an obnoxious sibling or an abandoning sibling or . . .).

Continue this prayer as long as you stay rested, relaxed.

If your alcoholic parent has died, you might vary the exhale prayer, saying: "Daddy (Mother, Uncle Tony . . .), I forgive you." Many ACOA have reported relief when they have talked through their feelings with a parent already dead. Direct address to a deceased beloved one of God is our privilege, thanks to the resurrection.

Parents alive and still drinking are more difficult not just to forgive but to deal with. Although alcoholism is a disease, tough love, a truly forgiving and honest love will have to stand firm against the alcoholic's patterns of manipulation. Al-Anon meetings are a most helpful tool in separating, without repeating well-worn behaviors from childhood, the disease from the person.

Parents alive and not drinking need our forgiveness, especially if they participate in the twelve step program of Alcoholics Anonymous. One ACOA remembered her father taking her aside at a family gathering. Active in AA, he was working on the ninth step, trying to make amends. Since he had been the loving but co-dependent parent in her childhood she had never been affected by his drinking which became abnormal only after she had left home. She dismissed his plea for forgiveness—until she learned how, by his co-dependency, he had betrayed her.

The co-dependent parent needs forgiveness too, but first he/she needs to be taken off the pedestal. Children who think in all or nothing terms tend to see the drinking parent as all bad, all dangerous, and the co-dependent parent as all good, all trustworthy—until, at some point, the co-dependent may betray our trust, overtly choosing the alcoholic over vulnerable little us. In our childish need to have one steady anchorhold we may have made our co-dependent parent into God. We possibly modeled ourselves after that parent so that our adult loving may be somewhat sick, not based on truth but on sentiment or duty or martyrdom or . . . As we discover more and more the truth of who we are and how we love, the more our parent-God can yield to God, the only faithful steady stronghold in whom to place all our trust.

Parents may be reading this book. These exercises in

hope for healing may help you, first of all, forgive yourself. You may be invited then to forgive your children who aggressed against you in passive ways or erupted in fury as they left home or who isolate you now, nursing their grudges at a distance. You may have to forgive your parents who taught you how to love from a skewered perspective and/or your ancestors who handed on the disease. More poignantly, you may have to forgive your alcoholic son or daughter for the trauma they are creating in your life, in your grandchildren's lives. "The alcoholic is a good person who's controlled by an insidious disease."

As ACOA you have been to your own Calvary, through your own passion. You may have relived it somewhat through this book, more consciously in union with Jesus. Our last prayer is for God's gift of com-passion, that we may share another's pain, bear another's burden, understand and appreciate another's way of the cross. We are invited to be instruments of healing. "Be you compassionate as your heavenly Father is compassionate" (Lk 6:36). Jesus not only urges that, but empowers us for that service.

Conclusion

In some ways these six steps in and toward grace relate to the twelve steps of Alcoholics Anonymous. The Twelve Step program is also applicable to other addictive behaviors, a real congenital weakness for ACOA. Some of us participate in AA or OA, Overeaters' Anonymous, or NA, Narcotics Anonymous, etc.—but some of us use the steps personally for healing our addictions whenever they crop up: a TV program, a friend's presence, shopping, long distance calls, bingo—whatever we think "we can't live without," whatever isolates us, ties us up in tension or guilt or just plain unfreedom.

Step one in and toward grace, "Awareness" corresponds with the open admission of AA's first step:

1. **We admitted we were powerless over alcohol—that our lives had become unmanageable.**

"Discipleship" entails the new learning from God, step two:

2. **Came to believe that a Power greater than ourselves could restore us to sanity.**

"Turning" is the meaning of step three in and toward grace, "Conversion":

3. **Made a decision to turn our will and our lives over to the care of God as we understood God.**

4. **Made a searching and fearless moral inventory of ourselves.**

AA relies heavily on human support too. Each member has a sponsor and finds a caring community in the AA meetings which they attend frequently. "Community" is reflected in:

5. **Admitted to God, to ourselves and to another human being the exact nature of our wrongs.**

"Union with God" mirrors the open receptivity in AA's steps:

6. **Were entirely ready to have God remove all these defects of character.**

7. **Humbly asked God to remove our shortcomings.**

and especially in the eleventh step:

11. **Sought through prayer and meditation to improve our conscious contact with God, as we understood God, praying only for knowledge of God's will for us and the power to carry that out.**

"Forgiveness" is the theme of steps:

8. **Made a list of all persons we had harmed and became willing to make amends to them all.**

9. **Made direct amends to such people wherever possi-**

ble except when to do so would injure them or others.

10. **Continued to take personal inventory and when we were wrong, promptly admitted it.**

and "Service" of AA's twelfth step:

12. **Having had a spiritual awakening as the result of these steps, we tried to carry this message to alcoholics and to practice these principles in all our affairs.**

As we draw to a conclusion, we hope that in some small way you have allowed the Spirit to establish in you a more trusting openness to God. We hope you know in your very bones that God does not want to hurt you or betray you. Now we ask you to try your trust with this exercise. Try to find a place alone or only with a very close friend as you work through this.

Ask the Spirit of Truth not only to guide you but to comfort you and make you strong. Remember and give thanks for all you have come to realize and for the healing begun.

Statistics indicate that as many as half the children of an alcoholic parent or parents contract the disease of alcoholism. We have looked at some of the other addictive symptoms that might occur in ACOA but none so potentially dangerous, yet so potentially freeing as alcoholism (or any other chemical dependency, i.e., drugs).

Invite Jesus right now into the room where you are reading this: as many as half the children of an al-

coholic parent or parents contract the disease of alcoholism. Ask Jesus to sit across from you and to
listen to how you feel. Take some time to let feelings
bubble up from deep within you. You, through no
fault of your own, may be alcoholic. Feel, and don't
censor your feelings. Jesus invites them all out into
the light . . .

You may rage at the injustice of having to live in fear
of whether and/or when the disease will strike you.
You may collapse in discouragement for, although
you have been careful about your drinking, a disease
is a disease. You may cry for your alcoholic siblings,
you may curse your parent(s). You may (and the
psalmists, with their cursing, complaining, laments,
model for us) say *anything* you feel to Jesus. Say it
again and again until the emotion has drained from
you. Let another emotion surface and repeat the
process.

Focus just on yourself and how *you* are feeling, not
on Jesus. He's just looking at you with such profound
tenderness, encouraging you to feel your feelings
and own them so that eventually you can share them
with him.

After you've said all you can, cried and raged and
trembled all you can, sit quietly for a while (probably
exhausted) and look at him looking at you. Then listen to him. How will he comfort you? Let him.

Jesus won't let you deny truth, so don't try to sweep this
danger under the rug. Alcoholism is in your genes in some
way right now. Even if you never take another drink (and we

are not advocating that unless you know you are alcoholic), alcoholism, like diabetes, may still appear in your children. If you swear off alcohol right now without the constant help of loved ones *and* the Lord, you may only be exchanging wet drinking for what is called the "dry drunk." Surely an ACOA group would help you be in touch with community and your "higher Power," as would Al-Anon if you are still living with or dealing with a drinking alcoholic. Total honesty with friends or non-dependent spouses and regular prayer for healing can also help you discern the truth about your own drinking. No one "answer" fits all.

Some ACOA we know, for example, liking their social drink, pray to be weaned from ever wanting to drink. Weaning, however, is God's activity, not our knee-jerk reaction to fear of alcohol. The defense of reaction formation has unfortunately led some ACOA to swearing off totally out of fear. Of course, if you are destructive at home or at work because of your drinking, you will need immediate truth and care. Ask Jesus to talk to you frankly about your drinking. Let him purify your head of old fears, of your need for the correct, the perfect. Then listen.

After a session with Jesus, check out with other people who know you how your drinking affects them. Some ACOA among those you ask might respond out of their own unhealed past with an alcoholic family. However, if some relatively free folks do have trouble with your drinking, ask them to be specific and concrete in pointing out incidents in which your drinking was dangerous, damaging or just obnoxious. If nothing is amiss now, ask one or two to shepherd you. For your shepherds, look for one or more persons who are themselves relatively free human beings. Shepherds do not count drinks or suspect every boisterous laugh. They are alert, however, accepting and loving you in an independent, not a co-dependent way. Ask them to let you talk about your drinking once or twice a year. *Not* too often! There is no need to let alcohol run your life now, all in the name of honesty. You will, in the course of working with this book, be thinking, feeling, praying a lot about alcohol. However, if you remain quite preoccupied with alcohol, check where the Spirit of Truth might be. The Spirit sets free, helps us let go of preoccupation, of any fear which may become an idol.

Remember too not to "strive for perfection" in forgiving. "Working through" this pain is a lifelong process. We will fail, regress. The greatest danger is to get discouraged and to close ourselves to God's desire to heal us. Forgiveness is not a once for all act of the will. Forgiveness is a way of life, a way we embody, despite our failings and regressions, the forgiving love Jesus offered, and still offers through us.

Do not shortly after your meditations with this book, or even during them, make major changes in your life style. These prayers will probably rile up the spirits within you and you need to discern carefully whether God's or some other spirit is moving you. ACOA have a tendency to impulsiveness, so don't "reach out and touch" an alcoholic spouse or parent just yet. If the desire to forgive is of God, it will not go away. Test your new-found forgiveness in small ways with other folk. "It is by their fruits that you will know them," Jesus explained. If your various relationships are becoming more free, loving, joyful, peaceful, if you are becoming more free, gentle and disciplined, then slowly, slowly trust those fruits (Gal 5:22) and the Holy Spirit. Try always to pray to the Spirit of Truth before doing/saying anything impulsively. It took years to be hurt, so allow, patiently (another fruit of Gal 5:22), time to be healed.

The healing of adult children of alcoholics is such a complex problem, painful in itself. We have only initiated *some* understanding, *some* helps for reimaging ourselves, our parents and our God. God is a mystery, infinitely knowable. Perhaps the healing of ACOA is not so much problem as mystery, infinitely occurring. Once God spoke right to the heart of our worst terror:

> Even if a mother forget her baby, I will not forget you, my _____ (insert your name). I have carved you on the palms of my hands (Is 49:15–16).

God continues to speak to us through the Spirit of Jesus whose hands have been carved with our pain, wounds to rejoice in, wounds streaming glory, peace, healing.

Bibliography

Becker, Ernest. *The Denial of Death*. New York: The Free Press, 1973.

Black, Claudia. *It Will Never Happen to Me!* Denver: M.A.C., 1981.

Brown, Christy. *Down All the Days*. New York: Stein and Day, 1970.

Burns, David. *Feeling Good: New Mood Therapy*. New York: Signet, 1980.

Canale, Andrew. *Understanding the Human Jesus*. New York: Paulist, 1985.

Edwards, Denis. *The Human Experience of God*. New York: Paulist, 1983.

_____. *What Are They Saying About Salvation?* New York: Paulist, 1986.

Ferder, Fran. *Words Made Flesh*. Notre Dame: Ave Maria Press, 1986.

Hall, Douglas John. *God and Human Suffering*. Minneapolis: Augsburg, 1986.

Linn, Denis, S. J. and Matthew, S. J. *Healing Life's Hurts*. New York: Paulist, 1978.

McConnell, Patti. *Adult Children of Alcoholics*. San Francisco: Harper and Row, 1986.

McDermott, Brian, S. J. *What Are They Saying About the Grace of Christ?* New York: Paulist, 1984.

McDonnell, Rea, S.S.N.D. *Prayer Pilgrimage Through Scripture.* New York: Paulist, 1984.

Satir, Virginia. *Peoplemaking.* Palo Alto: Science and Behavior Books, 1972.

Shea, John. *An Experience Named Spirit.* Chicago: Thomas More, 1983.

Woititz, Janet. *Adult Children of Alcoholics.* Hollywood, FL: Health Communications, 1983.

Yallom, Irvin. *Existential Psychotherapy.* New York: Basic Books, 1980.